Tidal

Published by Pine Row Press
Ft. Mitchell, KY 41011

ISBN: 978-1-963110-07-4
April 2024
First Edition

10 9 8 7 6 5 4 3 2 1
==========

Author's website at MARYDEANLEE.COM
Publisher's website at PINEROW.COM

Tidal

Mary Dean Lee

PINE ROW PRESS
Ft. Mitchell, KY

Table of Contents

Poems reveal truths. Sometimes they are also true,
or mostly true. Or not.

Part I

I fly across the street, over the dunes,
chase light at dusk and birds scavenging where the waves turn back.

Cardinal Flower

I know you,
skulking in the wetlands.

Red flash
beneath the boulder's shoulder,

under jack pine
and skeletons of cedar.

When I pull you up—
your grace drains fast

in a box
outside my window.

You must need something wild
I cannot provide yet—

you refuse to root.
Oh well. I'll just sit here, drinking

in your pure, red element
for a few hours

while you struggle
to live.

Sedimentary

Hair flying, dreadlocks
singed, she howls with
mouth so wide it parts
her face down the middle
nose collapsing to one side
eyes desperate for an exit.

She crumples into mud, rain
beating down, passes out.

Waking on her back
bottom of a river basin
under a shelf of rock
layer upon layer from eons
of wind chisel, ice scoring
water whooshing, grains of sand
re-crystallizing, cementing insect
appendages, banded iron ridges
pink-black compacted over time.

She remembers the bus that brought her,
how she got there, sees her flesh
hardening, thinning out, her crushed
bones becoming striations, her fingers
and toes tiny knobs, pieces of nail
catching the light, her hair a wave
cascading down. And then the mudslide
churns, catapulting down.

She angles her hand gasping.

Back Road

Beside a rail spur
the weight of kudzu
collapses tar shacks,
throttles trees. Acres and
chains of pecan groves. Shake
the trunks, nuts fall from husks
into mesh nets on the ground.
Small churches, smack-dab
in the middle of nowhere. Signs
for "1/2 price Sunday dinner with
a church bulletin in hand."
Purple, speckled, and
rust-colored field peas, crook-
necked squash, okra, peaches,
and scuppernong grapes
with leather skin, jellied clusters
sweet and tart
and everywhere,
boiled peanuts, their shells
softened by ocean brine
and heat like a wall
inside a room you cannot leave,
a rare shift of wind your
only respite, and at night it's
harder, hard even to breathe,
and in summer you can expect rain
every day, sometimes more than once,
and the steam to rise after,
and the whir of crickets and trill
of frogs to pause, no reason why,
then carry on.

Cousin John and I were Born a Month Apart

At low tide, we paired up to go crabbing,
me on the barnacles in old tennis shoes,
smelly rooster wattle on a string, fingers touching
the line, waiting for the tickle, John
scooping with the net,
dumping males in the bucket.

For decades, we did not talk.

Then John's mother died
and in the quiet of early morning, kids and a husband still asleep,
we drank sawmill coffee and recalled our mothers
and their passion for brown turkey figs,
how they would reach up to the overhanging tree

and pluck one, and peeling back the skin,
kiss that soft sweetness
made by cold water and hot sun.

That old fig tree died in a hurricane.
John and I went to a nursery and bought a new one.
But our fig did not thrive, and the following spring
we planted a third.

Then John drowned.
Our fig withered. Something in the soil had changed.
Its playful and curious secret of life was gone.
I think of him swimming so careless and deep
in the early morning.

Holding Electricity

Mother said holding hands with a boy would
light my breasts on fire, make my hips push out
like a roasted turkey. Fourteen, at the beach,
I was strolling barefoot at dusk, no one around
to see me smoldering, except my cousin John's
older brother Norman, sixteen, running his laps.

When he finished, he caught up with me,
asked if I wanted to go for an ice cream cone
at Flanagan's where John worked part-time
scooping dips. On the way back Norman took my
sticky hand and twenty snakes crawled up my arms.

Next night I told John I didn't want to go
to the library with him. Instead, Norman
and I squished our toes in the wet sand.
Just before the sea wall, he leaned down
and kissed me where I formed my words,
and where my legs came together, in the folds
a kite, a key, a storm that shook the world.

Night Music

Tall scrawny pines so close
the sun can't get through
quarter moon peeks at dusk.

You collect your cards
folding up your chair
go in.

Mother, you let me linger in the deep sill
no chores, scales instead
every morning.

You will charm Death
with homemade cinnamon rolls, a glass
of iced tea.

I dare you, cancer,
to dangle blame,
snap that cheap chain.

Frogs tuning up, how Venus is the first star
of evening. Teach me
a new riff, a sweaty stride piano.

Just Kids

We were five, then four, then three

ribs twigs snapped

                tubes to breathe and eat

      saplings spinning out

he's there but not —

one broken

              nodded off   into concrete

one swings wildly

                    strains to fill the gap

         blames   then   bails

father rows to his island

          I tremble

                  mother fills the jug

Driving Lessons, Baldwin County, Georgia

A dry Saturday afternoon, Dad presiding
next to me, I show off fluid clutch
and pedal, smooth shifting uphill
to edge of town—*How did
the debate go in civics class?*

I describe the heat around the poll tax,
beads of sweat forming on my brow,
a law meant to block black voters
by requiring a fee to get on the rolls.
I start to veer off the road.

He grabs the steering wheel.
Parallel parking is next.
I practice pulling up beside
a parked car. *How did the class
react?* How far is too far

before you start backing up,
turning hard into the curb, hear the
crunch of one vehicle hitting another.
I liked making the case against
the tax, even if I didn't win.

We drive to Dairy Queen. I tell him
about the fight in the hall after class,
the name they called me. The motor revs loudly.
He leans in, hand on the knob, *Clutch.*
My leg extends as he gently

gears down. Over malts, he grills me on stats
of county population, voter rolls by race.
Back in the car, we top the hill
above a ravine with no shoulder,
he unruffled, calm, my heart, pumping.

Seesaw

Long plank sanded smooth on a sawhorse
in the backyard. A rasher of cousins

clamoring for turns to match weights
adding and subtracting bodies,

sliding bums back and forth from the
endpoint, but someone always

derailed the long-sought equilibrium—
on a whim, jumped ship

or shoved another off,
sending the far end crashing.

It wasn't me.
My own antsy urge to disturb

came later—restless in love,
too long in a job,

I'd find myself on a bus
pulling out of town,

and send someone flying not,
knowing why.

My Namesake

After a day's drive south into the cloak of politeness,
telling Mrs. Thompson how nice her fruited chapeau is,
the funeral itself, a burgeoning buffet of fried
chicken and biscuits that would have given
Blind Willie McTell something to sing about.

Don't take the bait when talk shifts to integration,
remember instead the tamed wave of curls
on her head. Aunt Dean lived on a dirt road
I would skip across for lemonade and cookies,
her gentle pumping of the swing, and news of the niece
raised as her own. She practiced "Shall we gather at the river"
in the parlor, crimped strips of dough onto blackberry pies.
Her dining-room table set with linen, china and heavy glass.

Of course I loved her.

Slippery Rock

Halfway down a long, steep incline
there was a mossy patch that could
throw you off course, send you
toward the shallows. A parent often
crouched there to give a body a saving shove—
but nothing saved ripped skin on the bum.
Those who loved the place most showed up
with washcloths sewed to their swimsuits.

Slipping comes first. Looking away a split
second, misstep on the black, one more glass
of wine, sliding into the slide.

One camp-counselor-night-off, Peaches and I
cut loose from the drive-in crowd to see
if we could find the rock in the dark, tame
its slope by moonlight and land
safely in the icy pool at the bottom.
Waltzing down whooping and laughing,
we lost our shorts in the water, had to drive
back to camp, underwear sticking to vinyl,
our shirts off, windows down.

Quench

Alice filled jugs with the Oconee River,
swept the sooty hearth, baked sour loaves.
The hole in the tin wall, the rip in the roof
she took in amiable stride.

First baby a wild crawler always two sins
away from heaven, she scavenged wood
palettes, wielded hammer and cross-cutter
built a swing and sandbox in the backyard.

She saved the littlest from crushed glass and
mercury down his gullet, testing his teeth against
the thermometer. Grabbed the Ipecac and a sack
to make him vomit as she drove to the hospital.

Middle one crashed the car at seventeen, oxygen cut-off
too long. Five months in ICU: surgeries to repair face,
jaw, ribs, pelvis, breathing tube removed. Helped the
night shift after finding bedsores mornings, failure

to turn, her own hands dipping to clean infected flesh.
But the brain was stuck, messages locked in, some docs
advised giving up. She found a clinic in Philly doing
ground-breaking work, got him in, trained teams of five,

back home, three times a day, to lift and move limbs,
head. He made progress, then stopped—
She moved on, beyond empty arms, woke up
in the morning, went down to the Oconee again.

Gash Out the Gosh and Gimme the Gosh

Breech baby
stuck, holding on,
mother listening
to muffled rumble
of trains from the clay mines,
no one around able to cut,
release life.

By chance, a friend
of Uncle Bill's
was passing through,
a doc with a knife.
He delivered me
safe to whistle tracks
and tall pines.

Dad in the war,
we stayed awhile.
My grandpa Buddy
gathered giant cones
filling baskets,
tending fires
through the night.

A few years later,
Christmas in the big house
full of boy cousins,
I lay awake
long after bedtime,
tiptoed down,
found Buddy.

He took me with him
to check the fires
in the bedrooms—
up the stairs,
hand in hand,
plunking down
chunks of coal.

Then to the kitchen
for a snack. He melted
cheese in a frying
pan, divided it
on a plate
to share at the table
in the breakfast room.

Finally, to the library,
books floor to ceiling,
fresh logs burning,
rocking in his lap,
sucking an orange,
peels into the fire
hiss spit crackle.

Higher and Higher

Bill, enters high school at twelve, two grades ahead,
opens a tennis shop stringing and selling rackets, shoes, balls.

Bill, hits ace-serves, is the top-ranked Junior in the Southeast,
known as the come-back kid pulling upsets from 0-6, 0-5.

Bill, learns from Dad how to invest in the stock market, is tracked by
the IRS curious about "Lee's Tennis Shop" at a residential address.

Bill, dazzles at the piano, all technique, no sentiment,
startles the hall with crisp Bach played on the fast side.

Bill, excels in prep school, sent to recalibrate age and grade, unphased
by a bigger pond in the classroom, on the courts, graduates magna cum.

Bill, shifts focus in college—from tennis and good grades to girls,
dating, keeps notes in his journal on how to be a good conversationalist.

Bill, soars at an invite to be Honey's escort for a Deb Ball New Year's
in New York, but Dad won't pay for a trip middle of Christmas Break.

Bill, convinces his friend Ben to team up after exams, drive a Cadillac
New York to Miami for big cash so he can buy his own ticket.

Bill, borrows a friend's car in St. Pete for the last lap in tandem on the
Tamiami, then returning after the drop-off to all head home to Georgia.

Bill, arrives with Ben, after the 20-hour driving marathon, checks out a
campus party but can't find his summer fling Gail, crashes on a sofa.

Bill, pulls the Corvair onto the highway Ben and Caddy in his rearview, wings resting on his shoulders, breathes in the balmy air, window cracked.

Bill, starts to nod off, eyelids heavy, turns on the radio. The wheels veer off onto a disappearing shoulder, small bridge ahead.

"Car Hits Bridge Abutment, Youth Critically Injured"
Southwest Florida News, December 18, 1964

Piano

You moved in that summer—
a trial period, small room with a bed,
window. Ribs of black steel
pins of twine pulled taut
your hammers poised to strike
stretched strings a wide field of grain
lid a mink coat laid flat, its prop
a carved brown totem, releasing sound.
I worked on you five, six
hours a day—scales, etudes, and
Rachmaninoff's Elegie. My big-bosomed
Russian teacher pushed me to drill down
and extricate from you the purest wails
of sorrow and you let me. One day
looking out the window, I was drawn to
the tennis courts, where I met the tuba
player from the pit orchestra,
never looked back, no matter
how many times you called me.

Three Southerners

Amelia

Queen of the South, a single creamy flower
sits on a throne of glossy leather leaves.
Up close, she packs a punch
if you breathe in deep, naive.
One boy tried, broke two legs.

Flannery

Tiny white flowers poking up
top of the hedge,
emit a heavy waft
infusing neighborhoods
sweet tipping to nauseous.
Move fast or you'll pass out
she warned one boy.

Tanya

At night, tubes of furled lobes glow
like miniature flashlights nestled
in dense, heavy-veined leaves. By day,
velvet petals unfold, intoxicate.
You will think you're dreaming
she told one boy,
he never slept again.

Greasy Lake

Walking back from the movies
he pulled me into the shadows
of a side lawn. Kiss hard, tongue bitter,
a wondrous shaking inside me.

Before the next date, car keys jangling,
grandfather clock ticking,
I heard my father's measured Yes
to my being taken out in the car.

Out of town we sped to Plow Boy
for burgers, fries and malteds,
red and yellow jukebox.
I thought life would be like that:

scroll through the possibilities,
put in your coins, make your picks,
wait for the music of your life to swell.
As we waited for our records to load

we made fun of the other teenage couples.
"The Way You Look Tonight?" Please!
When our songs played, we sang along
quietly. From the parking lot,

he turned the car toward Greasy Lake.
A whistle blew, then clacking, waiting.
He made a U-turn back to my home,
kissed me again before I went in.

Dear Daniel

The spangled years we spent fighting
injustice—the striving, the songs,
the beatings, burned churches,
the back of the bus.

We got to know each other under fire—
Duke's first year of accepting black students,
five in a class of a thousand. We talked
late into the night after meetings,

your flock of NCC students,
my scraggly band of wild-eyed
radicals. You taught me how to deal
with the police and rednecks in the street,
calm an excited crowd.

Daniel, please write and tell me about your life,
how you are. Did you marry your homegirl
and become a minister? Do you still have dreams
about where we go from here?

Until a Female Appears

A whir spurs the search—
buckling the muscles beside their torsos
caving in where the ribs should be,
extreme deformity
snapping back, three or four

hundred times a second.
Small sac in their throats vibrating

and sometimes while waiting
they hug or hump whatever is near:
logs, rocks, trees, shoes,
until a female appears.

No, she is not blushing.

Bill

The years you lived after the accident—
unresponsive except for eyeblinks: one for *No,*
two for *Yes,* three for white haze over the breakers—

we all tilted as best we could to believe
you'd come back, wresting hope from
sporadic sparks of light in your eyes.

After five months you came home from hospital,
a patched dummy with glazed eyes, tubes
to breathe and be fed, with three shifts of nurses

scrabbled together. One night sitting vigil,
my hand caught a splinter from the wooden bedpost.
I wanted to be there if you woke up. Then I left

home for school, saw you on vacation,
made hospital runs at night to get icepacks
for high fever, your body in constant battle

with infections—kidney, lungs, bed sores.
When I couldn't sleep, I hung out, told
you about dancing to "Shout" with Dee

and what happened after. You
listened, I squeezed your hand.

What Do You Mean You Had a First Husband?

Peace Corps alum, "Best Legs" on campus,
takes me for Singapore Slings on my twenty-first birthday

in his Paris-green Cutlass convertible,
then tan lines, smoldering hues

in the empty auditorium where he listens,
the nightwatchman tells me,

as I practice Bach and Brahms on the Steinway.
He writes letters to me in Takamatsu—warm

and funny. He doesn't press me. I feel him in his words.
When I come home, he knows

how to make coq au vin. His hands are happy
in soil, patting down bulbs, bare back glistening.

I am still spinning,
rowing against my own current.

He smells of safety, knows how to weather
my squalls, gathers me in without diminishing.

One day, feeling lost, I walk home slowly
from the train. Marry me, I say.

Chocolate Souffle

Looking back, I didn't understand what
had to happen
        and then one day
I came home late, really late, Jim

steaming, me reeling from a single martini
on a dare with friends after work

and weaving my way to the kitchen, stumbling
through the steps of the recipe
                certain I was burning
the butter and flour in my tipsy state.
        I got it right

and when I approached the fragile folding
of whites into the sauce,
        I knew something
was different. They were meshing.

I'd never succeeded before.
When the doorbell rang,
        out she came,
perfectly pouffed,

my second generation feminism
ready to spoon.

Earth Day

After the protest two policemen on horseback
closing the park approached me and Vita

and offered us rides home. Sheepish but game,
we grabbed hold of their leather

and galloped across field and hill
of Fairmount Park. Gassed and smiling,

we waved goodbye. Jim was waiting
at the restaurant. I wanted to tell him

there's no heat in his hands,
his mouth, his tongue when we're in bed.

Instead I told him Vita had just
left her husband and two children,

that we'd ridden the night sky on
horseback through the park.

The day Vita moved out, she gave me
her grandmother's porcelain pitcher.

I fill it each May,
lilac branches with lavender clusters,

and I think of her waking up
to her new life.

You have to grab the berry
by its small leaves, she said,

dip it into sugar and cream,
then pop it quickly in your mouth.

To the Graveyard

My husband's out of town two weeks a month,
I'm churning out a thesis and pounding
tennis balls against a backboard. One day

I meet Peter, a friend's younger brother home
from school for summer. We hit some balls
then he suggests a trip to the Jersey shore.

We stare out at flatlands of cranberry bogs
till the bus drops us amid the chaos of children
and families splashing, building castles.

Later we pull out paperbacks, return to the waves
after egg salad and radish sandwiches.
Peter walks me home from the train.

I resume my spirited investigation of indefinite
articles in Chaucer's *Astrolabe*.

We tiptoe around when my husband returns.
His new love is a man. We can't move on.
I cry when he's here, am numb when he's gone.

Peter calls. He wants to show me something.
We bike to an old cemetery on a hill out of town.
We separate, walk around. Stars come out

lighting a smooth slab of stone. I lie down,
Peter finds me, sugar canes me, atop the dark words,
born and died, born and died, born and died.

Salt Marsh

I am the life blood of the marsh
continuous flow in the winding creek
between smooth cordgrass and black needlerush
buffer between sea and land—green, gold, orange and yellow

Continuous flow in the winding creek
pumping action boosts nutrient flux, collects detritus
buffer between sea and land—green, gold, orange and yellow
marsh grasses feed on my incoming waters, they give back

Pumping action boosts nutrient flux, collects detritus
alternate flooding and exposure enhance the crop
marsh grasses feed on my incoming waters, they give back
shimmer in sunlight, spurring new life and growth in the sea.

Alternate flooding and exposure enhance the crop,
generate nourishment for plankton, shrimp, mussels, clams
shimmer in sunlight, spurring new life and growth in the sea.
I am the life blood of the earth.

Second Street Morning

Tide is out, the expanse of sand is deckled instead
of bare beach smooth and level down to water's edge,

to mirror curling waves and curl of the ocean, a still life of rise
and fall, traces of wild currents scattering plankton, crustaceans.

Eyes on her feet, she picks her way across uneven surfaces, winces
at drops hitting her back, a tempest shower bears down, lets loose, ends.

She steps around scalloped pools of water trapped, shallow gulleys,
rivulets carved deep. Rain dots the veneer, reflects a rosy streak,

from the sun busting up from under. Low-lying clouds lift, purple
edges turn orange and pink against a grey-black canvas. Raising

her head as she reaches the sea, she tosses off her shoes, kicks
foam toward the horizon, only ocean between herself and Sierra Leone.

Somewhere out there is the boy who drowned when his lungs
filled up with her. Digging in with toes she plants herself,

takes on the slow rise of water, over her head, then floating,
paddling against the current to keep her place, watches the churn

and crash of breakers on the shore dwindle to quiet lapping.
She holds her ground from still waters to middle of the furor

to deep sea and ebb again, biding her time listening to
arcing dolphins squeal and whistle at catching mackerel.

You Held That Door Open a Long Time: Why Didn't I Go In?

A fine, young tree grows in Quebec.
I sit at the window:
slender branches and pale-green leaves
flutter, and

Wispy blonde hair, glasses,
you were twenty-two, a smart
Colorado ski bum. I was
looking for a place to taste Merlot.

You offered me a cushion against a painted wall
in a hallway at a college party.
Something about our floor conversation,
the way your hand stroked my dog.

I went to a free lecture with you,
then a deserted nature preserve—
only the creatures heard my reckless moans and cries.
You pulled me into your appetites:

sliding across white quilts of new snow,
signing the hotel register Mr. and Mrs.,
your lithe body beside a fire,
holding on, going limp.

Every morning in sun and rain,
the tree becomes different.
When it fruits I am ravenous.
You taste like raspberries.

What Do You Want?

I talked about the scarcity of female faculty
where I'd visited, wondered what that meant.

You're at your peak, he said.
You can go anywhere you want.

What do you want? he asked
again, slightly al dente.

What I want, I blurted, is to have a child
and a career, a life like YOU have.

He laughed: *No, not yet.*
You have to BURN, my dear—bear down,

publish, do nothing else
for the next four or five years.

I'd just turned thirty-six.
Happy birthday. Happy birthday to me.

Bottom of the Well

I stand poised ready to pump
rust-tinged water, pitch a few buckets
before getting to clean and clear to carry
across the April snow-covered ground.

The force of my arm on the stick, down
again and again, nothing comes up.
I look down and see empty, parched,
dried up lines and wrinkles, and

hidden in the depths, a rotting corpse,
a creature drowned by mistake
drilling a tunnel to meet his mate,
winding up in the wrong bed.

So now what, a contaminated well
ninety feet down—is there an option
to walking away, chalking it up, a new
well, drilling rig, fifty bucks a foot?

I peer into the depths with a special lens,
glimpse a red leaf fallen through a crack,
a baby frog trying to swim and leap its
way up and out. I telescope down into the

chasm to figure out what survives in the
black hole, how the frog keeps going after
fifty-seven times, and how to reach into
the screen to stroke a cheek, kiss an eyelid.

My thumb slides up and under the edge at the
lower left-hand corner, sinks into soft gel and
tumbles, back of my hand landing near his temple
while my lips open and fly to his smile.

Juicer

First came Valencias, still greenish
in November, their juice sweet and thin—
then Temples in December, a bit tart,
seeds galore. January
brought Honey-Belle Minneolas,
his favorite, one orange per glass—
and finally in March, small Murcotts,
red-orange, signaling the season's rapture.

At the sink early morning
he'd wash and slice in two
the number he thought
it would take for five glasses,
then press the halves one by one
on the ribbed cone with his left hand
while cupping his right against
the rounded back end of the
mix-master to control the speed.

My father knew oranges.
I can still smell the hot metal,
hear the hum of the motor
beneath the slushy grind of the reamer,
and hear the soft splat of pulp
riding out the spout,
hitting the side of the glass pitcher
as I waited in my school clothes for a sip.

Postcard from My Brother

Dear Sis—
        I think of you now and then
in the void I inhabit, still nineteen—

nothing to smell here, no ripples on water,
no endings, no playfulness, no seams—

and I think about her, too, the one I met
that summer,

holding her hand beside the rushing creek,
the letters that made me yearn

to drive all night to see her again.
I don't remember nodding off,

only silence.
        Sis, she is here now:
middle aged, timid, birdlike

still radiating that delicate beauty
from her cheek bones.

And you—my conscience, my rock,
my civil-rights mover, good daughter—

what pain, what solace has come your way
in the land of beginnings—

I want to see you.

River Stones

Degrees of smooth
and round

and different kinds
of rough,

holding fossil parts
and not—

apricot
mute grey

striped rust on cream.
Into the shallows

light bores,
        beneath layers.

The shadows find you
    no longer

among your sisters and brothers
but in raked sand.

I listen for hours, hope
to hear you.

The First Climber

The boy falls out of the birch tree splendid in sun
top of the upper meadow. Climbing higher and

higher, he grabs a rotten branch to step
into the canopy, catapults down, landing

headfirst on a giant boulder. No blood, no cries
but his eyes are dilated, his tummy hurts, they

admit him to Emerg to watch for internal
bleeding till morning. Released and fine, he's

twenty feet up a cedar by late afternoon.
He's bent on higher and higher,

not getting somewhere—like that day in the dunes
at Pensacola Beach, miles from houses or people,

just the four of us in February eating sandwiches
between two rows of high dunes, shelter from

a brisk gale to bask in sun. Finishing cookies, juice
boxes, suddenly he's gone. We call out, brush off

sand, hustle up the hill to peer around from the top: No
sign of anyone in the dunes, up and down the beach.

Not a soul, no other cars by the road. Silence,
except for gulls and terns, regular crash of waves.

Robert heads one direction, me the other, striding
up and down in soft sand, calling out. How could

he disappear so fast in this desolate expanse of blue
and white, white and blue to the horizon?

Part II

Rising cylinders of grace, I emerge from your vase
spilling over among the leaves.

Tidal

Porch to beach and back every morning
if we can find an older cousin to take us.
Towels on rails next to smelly conchs, sand dollars.
Shovels and buckets stacked by the screen door.

Down the stairs balancing on planks over the marsh,
holding hands to cross the road, breaking loose
at the soft gray soil, leaping over crawling vines
and sandspurs to get to the tabby steps spanning
the rocks and sea wall holding the ocean back.

Running on wet sand splashing and laughing,
toes scattering froth on waves slipping back.
Someone starts digging and piling,
packing dry sand, hauling water to drip the
outer layer, until Danny Boy lops off the top
of a tower and the littlest explodes in tears.

The tide is going out now, waves breaking
lower and lower, traces of broken shells,
seaweed and claws marching down the beach,
trips to fill a pail getting longer and longer.

We head home barefoot, forgetting the sandspurs,
burning hot pavement, while Aunt Melba stuffs
flip-flops in a satchel, yelling at us from behind
as we race to get to the shower first, rinse off
salt and sand, shake out towels, hang to dry—
till tomorrow, one more time.

One summer a plague of slippery black
muck erupts along the shore, small hills and
valleys that harbor sharp oyster shells.
No swimming, no sandcastles, no wading
in ankle-deep waves sputtering their last
hurrah. We try roller skating, bowling.

No logical, scientific explanation
or mention of hope for return to normal.
The next year and the next, no beach.

Learning to Ride a Bike

My brother Bill came to me
for love advice one summer. He'd
give me a play-by-play account after a
date at the movies and milkshake at
Dairy Queen, wonder if he was going
too fast, how to make the best first move—
arm against back of her seat (not touching),
lifting her hand as they walk, laying a
kiss on her neck in the shadows.

I told Bill: *Kissing is dangerous,*
you should play it cool. But he was
determined, thought maybe taking a girl
to a dance was a good move, could speed
things up, using a slow song to gently
pull her closer, feel her response.
My mind went to the heat of a recent
slow dance with Jack after a sweaty rumble
standing apart, his grip tightening low,
back of my waist, our centers of gravity
joining, his spinning me out in a twirl.

One night Bill knocked on my door
after another date with Sheri, asked if I was
awake. I was just pulling Jack out of his pants,
shoved him to get under the bed. *Go Away!*
Bill came in and plopped down on the twin bed.
thanked me for my advice, said it worked like a
charm to slow down. *We held hands in the*
movie, and on the way home I pulled her into
the neighbor's garden and kissed her on the mouth!
After he left, Jack wanted to resume. I opened
the window to ease him out on the hedge
tossed his clothes down to the lawn.

Iguana

I see you, Jessie, poking your finger
in the hole of the rain barrel
to stop the arc of water spurting
out, gathering lightning bugs on the lawn—

You are different from me—
trying to please, be the big sister—
I release you from what trapped me
in long ago sepia.

I could teach you tricks
for when the heart hurts—
humming and dancing
in front of mirrors, dark light
trickling through windows,
bare feet lifting up and
landing, on cold wood floors
that lead you out of Juniata valleys.

But you don't need that,
jar open, ready to pounce—
a great lizard, wreathed in scales
wanting lunch.

Woodstove

Coal black guardian and protector
standing in a corner, reddish cedar logs
behind. Angled feet belie your heft
as you hold court, knees bent, elbows
rising, lifting lattice shelves bracketed
by cast-iron splayed dragons, heads tucked,
tails curled, neck rising through the roof.

Winter morning, rasp of your steel doorknob,
clank of split logs against the floor
draws us from cold beds to add kindling,
smush in yesterday's quatrain, a haiku,
watercolors of sparrows, dried flowers,
then warm our clothes and dress by your side,
pulling up rockers to wait for your hiss.

Sky Valley Music Camp

Pianos for daily practice could be found
in the shed, the henhouse, the hay loft.

Mine in the horse barn,
hadn't a single working key,

so I fingered in silence, waiting to hear
myself play at lessons, twice a week.

Saturdays we danced with the boy's camp.
Violin, double bass and a caller kept us hopping.

When the band played "Waltzing Matilda"
or "Wild Irish Rose," at last slowing,

those lucky enough to have met someone
could feel an arm at their backs,

pulling them close, raise a hand up his shoulder
and collapse against his chest.

Each summer I imagined meeting my love there
pressing my nipples into his through our cotton,

feeling him press into my rose-tiered skirt
before climbing into the flatbed for the jostle home.

Tango with Moving Water

Light's soft ribbon undulates 'Round Midnight
a receding moon rising lopsided, spilling across the bay
beckoning me *come closer, deepen and swoon.*

Ebb-tide pool subtle quiver—a light breeze or
something trapped? A jelly fish, baby horseshoe crab
with its poisonous spire. My feet twitch for the warm
murky unknown, then pause, toes curled.

Mountain creek rippling pulls me in past the brush
rivulets against stones, rush of water. Over the brink,
rock-hopping across, sucking in my breath, each leap
a devil's dare: to arrive dry sneakers, pants legs and all.

River downstream sweeps me in, arms pulling,
dip and roll, smell of steeped cedar. Shoreline flies
till seaweed signals time to turn, shift to back stroke
battling waves, boat-wake swells, mouth and nose overcome.

Ice-cold shower of well-water freshly pumped and dumped
from heavy pails atop a deck, pitch under the stars.
Sweltering night of sweat slithering ceases, screams
and laughter echo out over Greasy Lake.

To the Son I Wish I Had

At seventeen, nailed Chopin and Bach
on stage in the limelight.

Fifteen, no words. Pimples.
Fourteen, you called me into your room
I waited, felt your ache.

At twelve you baked chocolate,
refused a bedtime check. I withdrew
ate my own brownies.

At nine you held my hand, unawares,
my feet lifting off the ground, showed me
your hand-drawn maps, cities and mountains.
.

At six, you dug in, we squared off:
no peas, no celery, fewer baths,
less piano. Only games.

At three you liked my bedtime stories
about Herman the hermit crab losing his shell,
fell asleep in my lap.

I almost lost you at twenty-six weeks,
twinge in the belly after tennis,
then lay motionless twelve more.

At nineteen, you left home.

Meeting Joe

We'd known each other just a few weeks
when you first introduced me to Snow Road,

your cabin in the woods, pungent aroma
of fresh-cut cedar, views out over the bay.

You told me about pouring concrete in summer,
stacking tongue-and-groove logs in fall.

By winter, under a post and beam roof,
you added wide-plank floors, a wood-burning stove.

River stone, smoothed from seasons before me,
I sometimes wonder.

I never saw your edges,
heard about lost loves, stolen chapters.

We slept on a mattress out on the deck
under the star-jammed sky, a loon

calling *make-love, make-love* from the lake below,
my arms and shoulders aching, blisters

stinging on my hands from canoeing
to the dam and back in rough, chopped water.

When I woke, you were already up
clearing brush to the limit of the woods
in your steel-toed boots, work gloves.
I watched you pick a lavender spire

before climbing the hill. Then you placed it
in a jar, made me coffee and pancakes.

Your laughter, your calm.
Where do they come from?

The Arc

I feed you, change you, pull on the snowsuit, tuque and mitts,
clean the snow off the car, drive to the studio, park, arrive on time,

hustle to undress you, settle you alongside the other babes,
unroll my yoga mat next to the other newborn mothers.

Five minutes in, you start to whimper, lacking love.
I want to run away to Minnesota where I hear it's warmer.

No, not my baby. I'm kicking hard to get some air just there.
Life, give me back my lungs!

I might drown but you're hungry.
I try to hold off,

hoping you'll go to sleep
until full-blown wails. I go to you.

You drink and dawdle, take your time on each breast.
Other mothers, postures holding, squirm and leak with your cries.

Summer Night in the Smokies

In the scant light and shadows
I wind my way to a stone house

hugging the mountainside
and a niece's baby

feeling the low ache of family—
rip in the tapestry

young mother run amok.
As the tree frogs' swell builds

green upon green upon green,
I rise, babe in arms,

top of the tulip tree
to find where these crooners

are tucked in—elbows of branches,
woodpecker holes, leaf stem edges

and how they make their deafening
chorus that surges

through arms and chest,
thrums my brain—legs against

armpits? exhale from nostrils?
tongues tickling vocal folds?

This babe and I find a place to curl up
on a branch for the night

to inhale, to inhabit
the soothing tones, slow crescendo,

the surround of sound in our veins.

Dad at 96

He has fallen asleep
in the middle of lunch, mouth ajar,
half-chewed rabbit morsel on his tongue.

The sight of visitors
triggers the old charm:
clear, beholding eyes, that deep chuckle.

Later, he pushes a button
and a steel apparatus arrives,
grabs and lifts him off to his toilet.

Confident words from years ago
wanting to be in control
of his own dying, not living

past a certain point of decline. Gone.
He wakes from a nap, cloudy eyes
oozing, lids drooping, garbled words.

We tune out and chat as if he's not
there. Suddenly he comes tumbling back,
sits up, voice steady: *I'm ready to go,*

what can we do? Shock and silence.
The doc can stop his meds. Is that what he wants?
Write it down, I'll sign.

My brother pulls out his guitar and we sing
"Alouette" and "Old Man River"
Play that piano like you mean it, son.

He stares out the window
as if from a train:
pine trees, a small meadow.

Black Christ at Calvary

When Dad died I found some letters from his sister Maryat
and a faded snapshot of her painting of a black Christ on the cross.

She painted it for Walsie, the woman who sold us fresh eggs and cream,
more a mural than a portrait. Bold colors, faceless soldiers,

children running around, people grieving. Christ's dark head
resting on his chest.

I wanted to find it. At a church outside Milledgeville
I met Walsie's son, ninety-eight years old,

who showed me where my aunt's painting had hung.
He said it got taken down during renovations long ago, was in storage.

There it was, brought out of a closet.
The primary colors, stark figures, the movement, the mourning.

My mother was a powerhouse, says Mr. Walker.
He doesn't understand why other church members

wanted to keep the painting out of sight.
Seeing it carries me back to my aunt's bold wanderings.

Mr. Walker and I were raised in the same town.
Here we are now.

Gathering Stones on Grand Manan Island

I pick up one at a time from the basin
an endless low stretch of sand that leads

to the sea. Each is larger
than a fist, cool to my touch.

I walk alone, weeping toward the hillside path,
two kids with father in the distance oblivious,

adding a few more till I can't hold all
but the weight feels good. I place them

in a sac of sweatshirt folds, tying of sleeves.
The first a smooth, triangular beige

his kiss a soft opening into a dark cave,
then a yellow round one with ink blotches,

asking me to stand taller, meet him at the
crossroads, the next milky and flat with arms

for holding babes, a tinge of rose on the underbelly.
I choose bigger and bigger ones, the load soothes,

begins to dissolve the knot in my gut, I hug
the pile close to my belly, feel the loosening

with each new stone, lift my feet higher and
higher stepping in soft sand farther up the dunes.

Channel

Shelf of hard ground, along the cliff shore
        in the cool air. The sun jolts
over the hill, hits like a spotlight—
    so direct and seductive I find myself stripping

then easing in, treading carefully
    on the moss-covered slippery stones
until far enough I fall back with a sharp inhale
        and float out

past the purple closed gentians waving near the shore
        and the young birch with leaves only at the top
then starting to swim to three cedar skeletons
        on to the cove beyond the weeping birch

up and down between the stump under the great pine
        and the dock upriver
and afterward tapering off, drifting to shore
        where I pull myself out

in the shadow of the fallen silver maple
            knocked over by my screams last winter,
collapsing on the warm spread-out clothes
            lying flat like a blanket, letting the

last drops evaporate, staying still for awhile
        listening to loons—until birdsong
signals my breast, I feel the wetness surge
            put on a layer or two and climb back up the monster.

Wild Remedies

Shepherd's Purse

Not a pocket for tools—
a whistle, a piece of rope,
its stem rises high and bare to the top
where heart-shaped pods collapse in a lump.
Perfect potion for vomiting blood
and nervous heart complaints.

Common St. John's Wort

Jam of tiny, yellow flowers
that last only a day or so
then turn soft brown,
fall off. Lime leaves
walk down the stems.
A teaspoon a day of elixir
wards off anxiety and the blues.

Northern Bedstraw

Always hovering at river's edge,
your roots and leaves make a strong brew
that stops diarrhea in its
tracks. You look like
your brothers and sisters
in the family of *Bedstraws*
—spare arrays of white flowers—
but I know enough to tell
you aren't *Fragrant*
or *Rough,* or *Wild Madder.*

Bladder Campion

A high-school farter in the stands
cheering the team on? Your
white flower emerging
from the pale-green sac
steals my breath and your juice
soothes burning and itchy eyes
like no other tonic.

Closed Purple Gentian

God, make me one. Let me appear
only at the end of summer
to hang out by the water
in clustered, puffy blossoms
that seem ready to open, but never do.
My great grandmother taught me
that 'gentian violet' is a miracle salve
for horse legs and elsewhere.

Full

Jessica arrives first, in time for acorn squash soup
and summer tomatoes, drags her heavy suitcase

always too full of stones for the long weekend, up the stairs
before heading out for a walk in the neighborhood

under trees fresh-turned, reds and yellows. We pick up
David later, lots of text updates to minimize waiting,

circling. He leaps from the curb, new beard around his smile
asks what's for dinner, then interrogates the kitchen, the fridge

for what's missing and not. I lie down for a nap
before supper, hear him chat in French with friends

on his cell, her singing in the shower washing
her hair, feel my torso lifting, filling with air, rising.

Their scent, their tall and lanky, the lilt in their voices
seeps into the walls, reverberates, the house is bursting.

Kitchen counters collect empty glasses, small plates
with crumbs, and post-it notes: *Don't forget to do your*

chin-ups, get a weekend Metro pass, begin yoga with a prayer,
order a Tarte Choco-Café from Bazin, oil the bike chain.

The day after they are back to their Brooklyns and Halifaxes,
the gingko drops all its leaves, yellow cloud on the ground.

Second Baby

Walking in wide circles around the room
watching your face, waiting for tiny eyelids to drop.

Your weight sinks into my back and shoulders—
I'm carrying wet clay now.

> *Mother where are you*
> *I want to give him back.*

No piece of the day was mine with you in my arms
fussing, eating, emptying me, picking me clean.

With my palm,
I stroke your limbs as you drink,

feel your sharp grip on my nipple
as we tune into the same distant channel.

A leaf-rattling breeze hammocks the trees
and we are swinging, *full swing*.

The Bird—

perches motionless, barely visible

      in the narrow channel's tall marsh grass

blue-gray merging with blue-gray-green

      in shallows cluttered with boulders

only curving neck, head, rump, horizontal line

      of beak betraying a skulking presence

unblinking killer scanning the flooded

      scrub thicket to fill its gut.

Fish pause in shadow, a bullfrog goes mute

      in mud flats nearby

until neck extends, long legs dangle from its bill

      wide wings lift and we are flying.

The Chair Electric

Springs shot, lumpy, it looks
like I feel: pain in the back,
a sumptuous lack in the wings.

I sink in, pondering where I end
and it begins. He plops down
squeezing in, nibbles on my ear.

We listen to wet piles slide
off the roof, the hum of big machines
plowing, clearing a panic of snow.

The chair played refuge for one child, sometimes
two, for many years. A place to read
bedtime stories, soothe unspoken

hurts, banish bad dreams—a place
to sing lullabies and camp songs
or sit quietly in late-winter dark

enduring the wide-awake hours.
Maybe it's time to let go or be replaced.
I sit here all the same—

its worn-out inadequacy soothes me.
Here, it's okay to feel hollow, spent
or used. Just being in the chair,

drawing in some buzz buried in the upholstery
amid faint odors and stains.
Even before our love making ends

he knows I'm going to fry him.
I make sure of that.

Season

A rolling rustle
from the meadow forest,

a fawn in flight bursts out, wolf
at its hind and I smell

the musky wind as horizontal
torso, long grey legs veer off toward Joe

and I am standing with my night shirt open, coffee grounds
still in their basket, too late
to shout, *Take me!*

At night the wolf returns,
finding me in a hollow
among dry leaves.

I wake and feel
Joe's loins along my back
and wolf-whisper, *Quiet, he's asleep.*

Outside I clamber on his back
and he takes me to a smoker of wolves
howling and carrying on.

I keep step, circling and grab a bone
to suck clean alongside the rest
and then race back home

leaving a deer tail on the porch for Joe
before climbing back in bed.

Second Climber

Decades later I pull myself up the birch,
gripping with knees and chest, grab the first

sturdy branch, surface rough, not a place
to sit, take a breather. A little further up

around the side? A limb parallel to the ground
looking out over the water, maybe? I reach up
to find a better spot, next rung, feel twigs snap
off against my jeans, but there's no view,

too much foliage, offshoots, branches woven tight,
maybe one more rung? It's like vertical bushwhacking,

less body surface to thrust with. As I move higher, snail's
pace, I focus on what's in front of me, what's in the way—

my husband, Quebec, Georgia.

What Can I Do to Make Things Better?

In his tuque, late October,
raking leaves in a boisterous gale,
tines raised high
to chase scattered yellow handfuls.

November, in his jacket—sleeves too short,
wrists jutting out—he scans the yard,
puzzles over a gangly gingko
across the road, which overnight
has dropped its leaves, become all bone.

Now December, he hangs sheets on the line,
clip and zing, sun skating low across winter.
Will the sheets soak up enough heat,
hold tight in the whip of the wind?
His vest is so blue.

April, in his flannel shirt out back
snapped-off tulip and daffodil stems
in the raw beds. He holds a rake
amassing lost colors and blooms

then breathes deep of Heaven, exhales what is not to be
and keeps working.

One night I break a china cup,
my grandmother's Florentine with turquoise rim,
while drying and putting away in a torrent of telling him
I can't stand it any longer, not being seen,
his simmering outrage at who I am.

He listens, keeps washing pots and pans,
wiping down counters, collects fragments
of the cup handle to glue back. I break
another and another and another.

Burning Off the Haze

One morning, a silent
blanket of beige fog hangs over the bay
like a chemical leak.

Maybe we should go into town—
take weeks of accumulated garbage,
overdue library books, restless kids?

Car loaded, windows cracked to lighten
the smell, Joe waves us down the lane.
Ninety kilometers, twenty-three books later,

waste dumped, groceries bought,
sun burns through the haze,
we pick up a hitcher along the way.

Spanish guitar on the radio,
my hair blows wildly in the hot air.
Fields flash by, the meadows scorched golden.

Jessie and David read nature books to the
back-packer and she tells them the blue butterfly
reminds her of the Sea of Cortez in mid-day sun.

One Nipple

My left started to itch,
crusty bits and blood stains
in my bra. The surgeon
prodded, studied x-rays,
probably eczema.

It was diseased, she reviewed
procedures, odds. I felt my babies
slipping away, their soft skin, their lips
rooting. And the taut wire vibrating
from bottle cap to pocket went slack,
road closed to the roar of waves. Flash
of a knife tapping my teat into a test tube

Had it been ignored, not gotten
enough sucking, licking? I tread water
through lymph node excavation,
partial mastectomy, radiation,
damage to tissue and muscle,
spasms of pain. Months later
able to swim laps, sleep through
the night, make friends with a
caved-in mound, less plump
on one side. Chatter between the
two about what's left, who's
more sensitive, the bitter pros
and cons of a replacement knob.

Thirty years later I'm up middle
of the night, reading a steamy novel,
one breast glued to the page, the other
glancing around the room uninterested
until it notices the cardinal flower
on a shelf. The nub rises and hardens
and the soft mound vibrates and
tingles as if to say, *Hello Dolly!*

Tour of My Heart

The upper right chamber is reserved
for my daughter

floating out the window into black night,
me holding her by the ankle,

my ears cocked for sirens, flashing lights.
The upper left

holds my feisty son
watching, waiting, fists ready

to strike what is invisible,
lunge at loneliness.

At the bottom
lies my husband,

arms and legs spread across
both chambers, pumping

fresh blood
in and out

of me. It's not
enough.

Blast Zone

Called home,
we take a new stretch of mountain highway

past blasted peaks and sawn-off hills,
red clay and stone still raw, exposed.

Bulldozers and warnings of dynamite
cede to midways with groves of redbud
glowing lavender-pink.

The tiny muscles between my brows fail to unclench.

Inside a West Virginia latrine surrounded
by flowering Seckel pears, a rickety woman with little hair

looses a deep cough. It echoes against the clouds.
I wash my hands a long time, dry them on my skirts,
return to the false safety of our buck wagon.

Joe clicks to the horses. Dolly and Blackie pick up a trot.

Letter

I write to you by hand,
form my letters, swoop and dive

on unlined paper,
shape and size words as I please,

imagine you in my arms,
rock all six feet of you in my lap

to shield you from the terror
and isolation, quiet your sobs.

I fold myself into the envelope, dampen
the sticky seal with saliva,

tongue to fingertip, and mouth
I'll be with you in just a little while.

I want to smell you close, stroke your
long silky hair, and hear you sing to me.

Naming the Hills

Fire in the stove, early September,
drenching rain and cold. Day after day,
trapped in the valley. Clouds render

our solar panel dormant, devices quiet.
Eyelids heavy, turpentine smell from logs,
we huddle in layers around the heat.

The eavestrough slows to a rare still.
Joe reads in a rocker. I lift my head.
From the rain barrel, a distant drip.

I grab my poncho, lace up my boots,
tramp down the muddy lane and lean
into the uphill stretch I call The Hump

to the top of Gulley Road. Dirt and gravel
replace pavement at Bullfrog Bend
as *jug-o-rum* bass notes drift off the marsh

before deer flies gather at Aster Strait,
paying no mind to weather. Cattail
Alley takes me through thick woods

to fresh scat along the shoulder,
my nostrils flaring as I pick up the pace
to reach the outcrop at Violet Harbour

of cow vetch, ragged-robin and bull thistle
before rounding on Farmgate Lane,
where the brook curves beneath the road

and wide-open fields unfurl. Time
to return, fiddle with radio static, learn
how many soldiers died today, how many lived.

Sister-in-Law Down the Rabbit Hole

She comes up from behind, hand
on my shoulder, I hear her laugh, turn
around to that mischievous smile, same
as the day I go home to meet my boyfriend's
family for the first time. His little sister, barely
five, takes me out to play in the backyard,
creams me with a packed snowball and I strike
back with a bigger, badder cannon ball in her
face with the force of my twenty-three years. As
she runs back to the house wailing, I am caught
between smug and mortified, desperate to return
to adulthood, wondering if she'll tell. Having just
lost two brothers, I do *not* want a sister.

We make peace after the marriage, but it's clear
I've stolen her main man, and she'll never forgive
me. Sometimes she lets me read to her, we walk
in the woods, kick leaf piles, make a racket. Last time
I see her, she's seventeen-going-on-twelve, refusing to
apply to colleges, won't look anyone in the eye. After the
divorce I wonder how she'll survive, wish I'd tried harder.

She and I meet up after all these years,
because Jim is dying, and we are rattled.
He saw her through solo treks—Appalachian,
Pacific Rim, finding her niche studying ticks,
mosquitoes passing on dread diseases, getting through
a thesis. He kept watch from a distance over my frustration
finding another mate, changing my mind about children,
a brother regained, taking a chance marrying a man I'd just met.

We catch up over coffee and muffins at a
diner off I-81 half-way between Syracuse and
Snow Road, Ontario, laugh uncontrollably about
getting hooked on clove cigarettes in grad school,
surviving a few quirky relationships, and complaining
about the impossibility of finding a decent carpenter.

And then there's Jim's feeding tube and walker, his partner
who's tuned out. He dies a few days later. *Now* we are sisters.

I Catch My Mother's Reflection in a Mirror

              heavy woman,

sloping shoulders in a man's plaid work shirt,

              expandable

maternity jeans, hair wild and woolly.

              I see the lines in your face

              around my lips

shoulders braced, jaw set

              to face what's coming.

              I feel your loneliness

hunger for more.

              Where is your smile,

the combed wave

              your pretty blouse,

              neck to waist?

Your mother

              when you have a child

blesses you with haunt and horror—

              What have I done?

Fantaisie Impromptu in C Sharp Minor

Sockets of pain in neck and shoulders build slow,
then seize, exponentially ring in my head. I arch

my back bracing for spasms—when a giant tapestry appears.
Thick brush of rhododendron in the Blue Ridge where I

got lost, a tennis court in a valley with sagging nets,
sun beating down on the match, receding into a corner.

Red and orange maple and oak against evergreens, crawling
through tunnels of low-lying cedar, tendrils soft on my face,

scent seeping in, pulling me deeper to find a cave for the night.
A figure wiped-out on a toboggan run, fingers and toes

almost frozen, dogs barking. Banks of azaleas calling me
home from Canada—lavender, coral, dogwood hovering,

wisteria climbing pines in the wood. Clumps of dark
clouds swirl in every quadrant, let slip daggers of lightning.

Oyasuminasai, snuggling on tatami with Kenji-san and Setsu-chan,
a dozen sleeping bags arrayed around *o furo* after a day of skiing.

Making *sashimi* on the Inland Sea, scales and guts dumped,
slices down the gullet, tasting salty on my skin, wet legs tugging.

I catch my breath, scramble across threads and yarns,
silky, velvet, coarse, scratchy—past the volcano spewing lava,

find a warm lake where I can float on my back, no current to
fight, little feet kicking my tummy, a song lunging up my throat.

I land in the lower left corner, a tightly woven valley—flat grey,
where a piercing headache strikes, deep cramps in my spine.

Sweaty blindfolds block the light. Hard to see from here the
splendor of the whole, subtle shapes and braids, labyrinthian paths.

Yet I hear the shimmering riffs unfold, collide, blow off steam,
subside. I let go, pull up the covers, sew myself in for the next track.

A Piece Breaks Off

Tall, scraggly life out back twists under siege, whip
of the night wind, heavy snow. From the dark of the spare
room by candlelight, I feel its sway, risk of snapping
brunt of the storm. It bounces, a dog leaping back of its knees

to bring it careening down. Vertical sheets of snow fly by,
now the spruce is walking, arms and legs lift on off-beats,
shake of a tambourine one side, subtle flex of elbow
the other. Hip slides, circling to tail bone, exuberant!

The gale sputters and halts, boughs freeze and brace
to hold the clumps of snow piled. Bare branches low
on the trunk reach out, shivering. Shoulders drop, foliage unfurls
and whirls a skirt around the bones. The old shepherdess

bends, regains her footing, spreads her warmth, ear cupped
for the return of Norman's drum and oh the drumming. Oh.

Canadian Shield

*Roads were constructed and crews of labourers hacked and slashed
at the forest, blasted at the surface rock in an attempt to establish
footings for the foundations of new buildings.*
—Alistair MacLeod, *No Great Mischief*

Jessie and David played in the hammock.
Joe and I hung swings from a beam wedged
between giant pines, cleared brush,
felled trees by the water for a dock—

a place to swim, jump, dive, float, catch eels—
and then engineered a way down the steep hill
to the shore, a switchback trail through the woods
along a rough staircase made of scrap railway ties.

Pumping slow water from a well-hole
quieted us and kept us strong carrying
water to the cabin. Inside were two small
bedrooms, one for us, one for the kids,

and the main room, windows looking east
to the rises. After a child's dream or my own
restlessness, I slept on the couch under a
red-orange crocheted blanket, dim kerosene light

until woken by the sun elbowing up
the opposite shore turning the walls
blood-red. No diapers, no chores, no one
to check on yet, red fading to white light

reflecting the river's ripples. No crying, no noisy
fishing boat, or the dog barking mad to be let out.
The house not yet come alive.

Wherever this is, let me stay longer.

Leave Over

My babes swing silently in the cool, damp air.
There is no one else here

on the tennis court, on the cinder track, on the playing field.
No other children in the sandbox, on the jungle gym, seesaws, slide.

I stand behind and push, watch their heads in the breeze.
Suddenly I am cradled by the stillness of this late summer morning.

I am rising and falling.

I don't want to go back to the world,
to running its races, to untying its knots.

The swells are coming every seven seconds,
teasing apart my tangled locks.

My Blue Cup

after Elizabeth C. Herron's "Blue Cup"

Drowning in the blue cup
yellow trees late afternoon in November
dissonant pause in a Reykjavik chorale

The blue cup is full
teetering on a tabletop towel
could tip any moment—fall
sloshing its nectar somersaulting down

Its blueness calms me lets me
have my fill of water and sky
sailing to sleep in my mother's
arms lullabies till morning

Drowning not dying—going underwater
holding my breath a long time

Afternoon Rally

I had no interest in easy banter
after a failed marriage and a long affair

but both of us liked tennis,
lifting the yellow ball.

Early summer, maybe a Saturday,
we met, new cans of Spaldings in hand,

waited for a court.
Once we began, the rallies

were long, he could place
shots anywhere, run me

up and back or pamper me
with a steady pace, predictable hop.

Deep to the baseline, drop
shot, crosscourt, down the alley.

The pounding of the ball, power in my return
reverberated inside and a fire began.

Playing my equal was a high.
I wanted more.

I invited him
up three flights, laughing and joking,

elevated heart rates. He didn't ask about
my thirty pots of cardinal flowers in the

living room on tables, the floor next to
windows, tops of cold radiators.

In the kitchen he helped defrost a
can of lemonade, touching my shoulder

now and then, and my nose brushed his
salty neck getting ice from the fridge.

This is ridiculous, I thought.
He's someone I hardly know.

Then came a tentative arm
pulling me close, lips on cheek

and breath in my ear, kissing, heading
for the sofa, clothes off.

*

Eyes open, spent, with sweaty limbs
I faced him in the light

and wished to return
to decorum, civility and coverings—

to converse as work friends
about nothing.

When he left, I took a shower.
Retreated to my rocker,

replaying, regretting.
Yet I treasure the choice,

when to pluck the ripe plums
or leave them on the bush.

Nebraska

In my rearview, dangly earrings,
gold chains, hair elastics
pieces of face—chin, jaw, ear—
snatches of blonde ringlets, cropped waves.
Images shuffle like a fast-moving deck of cards,
digital flipping of snapshots, fragments
of sea and sand-smoothed glass,

I sometimes catch a glimpse of someone
missed along the way, wonder if I could
stop, roll down the windy and say *Hello*.
What if I'd stifled that shout, reached out with a hug,
worn the dusty-rose instead of the yellow panties,
answered his letter. Would sound still come crashing?
Would I still be driving to Omaha?

2040

I'll likely be expired by then,
                    transformed, maybe

          into a will-o'-the-wisp
     floating in a marsh by the sea.

I wonder how I'll go
          alone, or not—
                    in a car,
     by drowning, fall off a cliff

          slowly rot
          from some common pox that preys on elderly Goth.

Or will I curl up like a cat
     purring at my mother's feet
          as she rocks beside some heavenly fire?

Maybe I'll pass my last years with my daughter
     planting lupines in the valleys
                    and at the side of roads.

     And then I will paint them.

I will take up square dancing,   easy steps coaxing me along
     for an allemande left, swing your partner,

     old codger grabbing me by the waist
steadying my crumbling knees and flat feet.

As I commune with the moon,
     sail off in my hammock to become
a loon's mate in the bay
                    Joe will hear me and understand.

East Beach

We gather to remember my brother's life.
Nineteen short years, told through letters and postcards,

and the story of my mother, after the crash,
trying to bring him back. I hand out bound copies of *About Bill*.

At the end of East Beach, where Postell Creek winds into marsh,
sandpipers' skinny legs move triple time.

The next wave rolls in. Coquina clams burrow.
Terns scan for bait in the yellow spareness of evening.

A porch door slams, a pelican
lifts with laborious grace.

I lay down in the pale-melon light
as a little protesting voice dies out.

Against the erasing tide, my sand shape changes
from imprint to afterthought to nothing.

Out on the bar, a trail of haze
over the *blinking* white breakers,

signalling yes, no, yes, no, yes.

Acknowledgements

Versions of poems in this manuscript have appeared in the following publications:

"Cardinal Flower," *Montréal Serai* and *What Lasts* (chapbook published by members/authors of the Two Susans Poetry Circle).

"Back Road" (formerly "Back Roads of Georgia") and "Postcard from My Brother," *Event*.

"Cousin John and I Were Born a Month Apart" (formerly "Cousin John"), *The Tishman Review*.

"Just Kids" (formerly "Riddle"), *Grain* and *Best Canadian Poetry 2021*.

"Driving Lessons, Baldwin County, Georgia," (formerly "Driving Lessons, Georgia, 1960"), *The Halcyone*.

"Piano," *Burningword Literary Journal*.

"Dear Daniel," *Salvation South*.

"Earth Day," *Ploughshares*.

"Postcard from My Brother," *What Lasts* (chapbook published by members/authors of the Two Susans Poetry Circle).

"River Stones" and "Season" (formerly "Cold Blue"), *The Write Launch*.

"Woodstove," *Broad River Review.*

"Meeting Joe" (formerly "Joe at Snow Road"), "Canadian Shield" (formerly "Morning Interlude"), and "Night Music" (formerly "On First Learning My Mother Had Cancer"), *Hamilton Arts & Letters.*

"Summer Night in the Smokies," *I-70 Review.*

"Black Christ at Calvary," *The Ekphrastic Review.*

"Gathering Stones on Grand Manan Island," *The Fiddlehead.*

"2040," *LEON Literary Review.*

"East Beach," *Dunes Review.*

Thanks

Thank you to my mother, Mary Dean Lott Lee. You loved me so abundantly and fiercely while not holding on.

Thanks to Alice Williams for being moved and telling me to keep writing; Jim Oliver, my ex, for teaching me to laugh; Michael Gerlach who kept knocking at my door; and Vita Laume, my poet friend before I became a poet who kept sending me books of poetry by authors she loved and I'd never heard of.

I'm also grateful for a few dazzling moments in my life: earning my *ikkyu* rank in Kendo under the tutelage of Kunikane-san and the Kendo Club of Takamatsu Dai-ichi Kotogakko; performing Bach's Partita #1 in B-flat major and feeling the audience in the palm of my hand during the *Sarabande;* rehearsing and performing the *Andante* movement of Mendelssohn's Piano Trio No. 1 with my musician friends, Catherine Walker, cello and Minda Bernstein, violin.

I want to thank Derek Webster and his workshop through the Quebec Writers' Federation in Montreal. I especially appreciate his guiding and educating me with sensitivity and patience.

Thanks to members of our Two Susans Poetry Circle who are an ongoing source of support and valuable feedback. I'm also grateful for my writing partners during Covid and beyond, two mighty poets, Marisa Gelfusa and Wren Jones, who have inspired me with their writing, triggered many poem beginnings with prompts, and kept their arms around me during roller coaster ups and downs.

Thanks to Barrett Warner for prodding and pushing, sometimes gently and sometimes not, and for shocking and confounding me, leading to generation of new poems breaking new ground, as well as important shaping and tweaking to put the manuscript into publishable territory.

Without the support and love of my family, this book would never have been possible. Thanks to Joe, Jessica and David Smucker for their enthusiastic embrace of my consuming and crazy passion for writing poems at this moment in my life, and for being the amazing individuals they are!

About Mary Dean Lee

Flowing near the Okefenokee, soothed by train whistles,
tracks rattling beside miles of slash pine.

Raised with cousins, summers on barrier islands,
conch harvesting, riding waves, and the tides
stirred by pounding and flashes in the sky.

A wicked arm-wrestler, torch singer, believer
in changing the world. Wound up in Montreal.

Professor, researcher, complainer.

I should tell you about being a mother,
because it's important to who I am and to
my poetry. But I will say nothing.

I fly a scarlet kite with yellow tail-feathers in high
winds, not afraid if it lifts me off to Timbuktu.

I ride my bike to the market for beans and corn,
oak-leaf lettuce, acorn squash, Quebec straws and blues.
There's a little bell on one of the handlebars that I have never rung.

www.ingramcontent.com/pod-product-compliance
Lightning Source LLC
Chambersburg PA
CBHW051323120626
46547CB00015B/2366